AutumnLeaves

Seema Jha

author HOUSE®

AuthorHouse™ UK Ltd.
500 Avebury Boulevard
Central Milton Keynes, MK9 2BE
www.authorhouse.co.uk
Phone: 08001974150

First published by AuthorHouse 3/1/2010

ISBN: 978-1-4490-3008-7 (sc)

This book is printed on acid-free paper.

Dedicated to my father
Professor Surya Kant Mishra

The thriving tree

Pulling himself from his bed
He looked at the day ahead
Got dressed for work
While a tiny thought lurked
He did not cry
But slowly he sighed
At office he dutifully did his work
His responsibilities he did not shirk
But all day he felt a sense of dismay
It was his birthday
No lovely dishes, no sweets would he get
No one would caress him, no one would pet
Not long ago, his mother had passed away
Leaving his world grey
He decided to go to a campus
And caught a bus
His childhood had been spent there
In the presence of his mother who cared
His mom had made many friends there
And now she was Lord knew where
Then they had moved to another place
And time had ruthlessly raced
Coming to the campus made him nostalgic
The happy past and then the end somewhere else tragic
He went to his mom's friend's place
His mind with sorrow ablaze
His mom's friend welcomed him with joy
Saw the man who had been a boy
Hospitality itself, she went to bring food
Leaving him to brood
After fourteen years he had come back to this place
Of his memories there was many a trace
No present from his mom this year
He held back his emotions, held back a tear
The lady came back into the room
In a matter of minutes, quite soon
She put a 'mausambi' fruit on the table
His mood had become a bit stable
"Your mother had given me the mausambi seeds
And now you should see the thriving tree
There is more juice than we can manage to drink"
Suddenly he saw the link

Those seeds had been given several years ago
He looked at the fruit's wonderful glow
"Eat it," she said
Adding lovingly, "Go ahead"
He looked at the fruit for a while
Then he slowly smiled
This was a birthday present
From someone who was not present

The Gate

I opened the gate and there you were
The leaves above seemed not to stir
Amongst your friends you stood handsome and tall
I admired your courage, I admired your gall
A hush fell upon you and your friends
Your conversation seemed to end
For glaring at girls was your pastime
And I was a teenager at the time
Were you ever attracted by me
Could there ever have been a 'we'?

I opened the gate and there you were
Everything else was just a blur
It was drizzling I remember
Was it July or was it September?
You took the trouble to look at me
My shaking heart danced with glee
I remember that day like yesterday
I remember I was wearing grey
Was it an accidental glance
Was it just a matter of chance
 I felt raindrops falling from my cheeks
I felt vulnerable and weak
Was it wrong to hope, to dream
Was it wrong to smile, to beam
Was the presence of teardrops wrong
Were the overwhelming emotions wrong
Did I repel, repulse or entice
Did I somehow arouse your vice
Was my so- called love a lie
Did I awaken in you a sigh

I opened the gate and you weren't there
All that welcomed me was despair
I missed you like one misses one's morning tea
Nothing mattered, the lovely sky, the dancing trees
It wasn't just our creed, our caste
It just wasn't meant to last
It was presumptuous of me to assume
That you were singing to my tune
A wall of arrogance hindered us
And we were separated thus

I was desolate, I was shattered
Whose pride it was, does it matter
I did not know, I wasn't sure
Whether my pain had a cure
You were a charming prince
Whom I had loved for my sins
Were my feelings reciprocated
Was I loved or was I hated
Had you felt even an inkling of desire
Had I imagined your burning fire
Or were you just an incorrigible flirt
Chasing madly after just any skirt
Were you my awaited sonnet
Or were you just a bee in my bonnet
Had I perceived more than was actually there
My stormy passion did you also share?
It is my secret woe
That I shall never fully know
Yet the truth might be too harsh to face
I'd rather not know till I enter my grave

I open the gate and you are not there
I've convinced myself I do not care
This is a gate and that was one
All that happened is dusted and done
Land and seas separate us today
Does it matter if it's sunny or grey
Does it matter if it's December or May
My hair is in total disarray
I haven't bothered to comb or groom
I haven't bothered to lighten the gloom
As I do all that I ought
I console myself with the thought
Why be sad, why be glum
When you and I share the same sun
Why should I despair
When you and I breathe the same air
We share the same earth, you and I
Surely that doesn't mean good bye

I open the gate and you are not there
Do I miss your tousled hair
Do I miss your impish grin
Can my memories of you be described as a sin
In God's court can I be pardoned

For remembering you watering your lovely garden
For remembering those eyes through the hedge
My so- called love led me to the edge
The insanity that has plagued my life
That has caused me pain, caused me strife
Could it be love and love alone
In a repressed society, was it my shrieking tone
Perhaps I was never crazy at all
It was in love a maddening fall

I open the gate and you are not there
But I do not wonder how you are and where
For I have heard on the grapevine
If ever you were, you are no longer mine
You are happily married, it seems
I don't begrudge you your joy, I'm not that mean
But somewhere in my heart, a dull ache persists
You're in the fog of my eyes, you are in the mist
You are there in the Indian monsoon
You are there in the romantic moon
Were you just an amorous hiccup
Was it just a storm in a tea cup
Was there more to it than meets the eye
Do they matter, the hows and the whys
All that matters is I felt what I felt
Does it matter if your heart did melt
It was an experience of a lifetime
It hardly matters that you are not mine
My love is pure, my love is sublime
It will transcend boundaries, it will transcend time
I want you always shrouded with mystery
You, who are now my history

Grief

My grief is loath to say good bye
It creeps in slowly saying hi
A menacing grin on its melancholy face
It pesters me in a thousand ways
Here I am again, it says
Come to darken your sunny days
Here I am to make you cry
To see you squirm, to hear you sigh
I am here in the lump in your throat
I am here, you better note
I will keep coming unannounced
Any moment, I will pounce
You will hide me somewhere deep in your heart
Try your best that our ways may part
But I am not one to admit defeat
I am cosily sitting in my seat
Why don't you accept me as your own
Why don't you acknowledge my alarming tone
Why don't you confess that I am you
And all else is just not true

Content

Is it okay to be mediocre or should one shine
Is being average such a crime
Is it okay to be of the ocean just a drop
Or is it necessary to be on top
Is it okay to do reasonably well
Or should one excel
Is it okay to be an alphabet, not a word
Is it okay to be just one amongst the herd
Is it okay to be easily content
Or is it ability perhaps ill spent
Is it okay not to achieve any fame
To be anonymous and not a name
To be brilliant, just fine
Or does one have to be almost divine
Is it okay to be not a gleam
To be in the kingdom, but not the queen

Autumn Leaves

All that gold on the ground
That amazing magical sound
Separated from the mother branch they lie
Looking gorgeous even as they die
Once soft, now they are crisp and hard
The life in them spoiled and marred
A poignant sadness overwhelms me
As I step on autumn leaves
The branch and the leaf have a link
But the leaves will rot, perhaps even stink
Is their relationship then lost
Will their paths again cross
When even the branch goes the way of the leaf
There is still no cause for grief
For the link will always be there
The link is alive in an empty chair

Serene

The garden is covered with a sheet of snow
I look at the white shimmering glow
While I was asleep in my dreams
Quietly emerged this picture serene
Softly, gently snow must have fallen
Nature's thunder nature has stolen

Steady

Steady, my racing heart
Don't you start again, don't you start
Pessimism will get you nowhere
Dare I hope again, can I dare
This happiness after troubled times
Can I truly call it mine
Will too much joy arouse an evil eye
Shall I smile too much lest I cry
O! Panic, perish, welcome the bliss
Accept this as destiny's gentle kiss
There is no reason to fret and fume
There is no reason to assume
If my highs are here, can lows be far behind
Be still, my worrying mind

11

Calm

If you will, call me silly
But I bought these artificial white lilies
I put the lovely flowers
In a white vase
And looked at my living room
My friend would be coming soon
I scrubbed my glass table
Which is supported by white angels
Cherubs rather
I gather
It went well with my so called décor
On the mantelpiece, a figurine no more
She walked in
And I grinned
'Those look nice
Pleasing to the eyes
But white lilies are used for funerals
Although that shouldn't be your hurdle'
The association of white lilies with death
Made me hold my breath
I looked at them in a different light
Suddenly they didn't seem so bright
What a shame
That white lilies have a sad name
That such calm beauty
Has such a painful duty

Raindrops

Raindrops on the window sill
Raindrops on the grass so still
Raindrops on the tall green trees
Raindrops on the many leaves
Raindrops on the window pane
Raindrops on the many lanes
Raindrops have given nature a shower
Raindrops are there on every flower
Raindrops on the hopping frog
Raindrops on the running dog
Raindrops on the little boy
Raindrops on his tiny toy
Raindrops raindrops here and there
Raindrops, raindrops everywhere

Page

Forget him, just forget him
Forget him as a passing whim
In a blink
In a wink
Forget his style
Forget his smile
You belong to different worlds
The mere idea is absurd
Forget his glasses
A crush passes
Forget his chivalrous ways
Forget his interested gaze
Unnoticed this feeling had arrived
Take care that it doesn't survive
Forget the quick beating of your heart
Don't allow this feeling to last
Boundaries you musn't cross
Make it a mental victory, not a physical loss
Forget him, just forget him
Forget him as a passing whim
Forget him as a fickle desire
Forget him as an unlit fire
Forget him as an idiotic dream
He might not be all he seems
Forget his voice, forget his words
You belong to different worlds
Forget not that you are spoken for
Forget not the stamp of law
The ring in your finger is a bond
Ignore all other fish in the pond
Forget him, he's the voice of Satan
Forget him, for you he'll be fatal
Forget his distinguished look
He is not a page of your book

Subdued

The colour green
Is serene
It is gentle
Like a petal
It is calm
It is a balm
It is soothing
It is alluring
It helps us breathe
It is sweet
It comes in several shades
And it gives us shade
Understated and subdued
It is never crude
Subtle is its beauty
It softly does its duty
The colour green
Isn't a blinding gleam
It isn't a storm, it is a breeze
It's in the leaves, fields and trees

Fragrance

Come into my arms
Unleash your charm
Smother me with affection
For I can't take rejection
Overwhelm me with the fragrance that is you
Overpower me with the smile that is true
My promises I will keep
Your love is pure, your love is deep
Come into my arms
Unleash your charm

Fickle

The flurry of elections is not unknown to us
The hustle- bustle, the enormous fuss
Elections are announced
Victors are pronounced
Grabbed is the coveted chair
Causing someone great despair
The loser might declare tongue in cheek
That the victor's personality is weak
Or words to that effect
For of power he is bereft
It is the loser's whispered shout
Of the victor's policies he has doubts
The rug has been pulled from his feet
It is always tough to accept defeat
Power like wealth can be fickle
Once powerful, you can end up in a pickle
Power is a strange thing
Joy and sorrow it brings
Power has charisma
It can be an enigma
Charisma has power
It can make a star
Power's fascination
Isn't lessened by assassinations
Power is a strange mistress
It can cause distress
Absolute power corrupts
It can disrupt
People with power
Look better than they are
Some women are dazzled
By men in the saddle
Power of the gun
Perhaps needs to be shunned

Norms

The English bride dressed in white
Quite a becoming sight
Starting a new life
In the form of a wife
The Indian corpse covered with white
Signifying the ebbing of life
Culture in its many forms
Defining our social norms

To you, precious

I assure you, my son, you are dear to me
Surely you see that, surely you see
I miss your lovely smile
I miss the miracle that is my child
I miss all your witty comments
I miss the support to me you lent
You are a flattering image of mine
You are a present divine
You are a fulfilled dream
The earth to me you mean
My sorrow's remedy
You are a sweet melody
I haven't seen you for quite a while
I miss the miracle that is my child
I miss your eyes, your lips, your nose
I miss your fingers, I miss your toes
I miss your laughter that fills the room
I miss your chats about the moon
I miss the sharing of news with you
I miss your carefully thought out views
I miss your presence in your empty room
Your teddy seems to sense the gloom
In your field, may you attain a high stature
You, who share my love for nature
You are the apple of my eye
From your nest you will fly
You are gentle rain
You are all that is sane
You posses the right
To set me alight
You are so tender, gentle and mild
I miss the miracle that is my child

Clan

My bitter half is watching cricket
Muttering "leg before wicket"
I toy with a crazy thought
What if in the midst of a shot
I change the channel
Risking his furious dazzle
I hear a crunch
Crisps are being munched
If only such passion I could arouse
We would have fewer rows
With ignorance I am stumped
For understanding I hunt
I feel I'm on the pavement
Devoid of my fashion statement
Awareness of cricket has become the in thing
I inwardly lament and whinge
Totally detached
I hear the gloating "catch"
It seems weird to be obsessed
In every move to be enmeshed
The subtle nuances are keenly observed
In memory, quietly, firmly preserved
To be flaunted at leisure
At a game seizure
As if keeping score wasn't bad enough
The going gets even more tough
Afterwards, every second is analyzed
Every little detail is prized
And if I dare say "It's only a game"
He seems to undergo severe mental pain
Devoid of interest I emotionally bleed
After all I am a dying breed
Perhaps I should join the fans
Maybe I should join the clan

Allure

The sheer poetry that is you
Is stealing hearts quite a few
For one thing is for sure
You haven't lost your allure
Life has given you your share of sorrow
But you look ahead welcoming tomorrow
It seems tulips, roses and daffodils collide
To create such warmth which is difficult to hide
Your magic takes my breath away
In November you are the month of May
You've just arrived on the stage of life
May you prosper, may you thrive

Mr. Obama- The President

It was a situation grave
When your ancestors were slaves
Their black skins were frowned upon
Yet you gave rise to a new dawn
Unipolar is the world, America the king
Yet you are down to earth, devoid of wings
For you, the climb has been tough
For some, you are not black enough
You are reassuring in many ways
In the quivering economy, you're a sunny ray
To the third world you will give aid
Of money they desperately crave
I know that you really care
I know you know that it isn't fair
To light a single lamp in your room
When all around is darkness and gloom
You will not be inhibited by boundaries
You who are out to create history
A man of your intellect appreciates
Fanatics are out to destroy and hate
May you win over foe and friend
May terrorism come to an end
With a sensible head on your shoulders
You will overcome all the boulders
May be it is too optimistic to hope
That with every problem you will cope
For some conflicts have no answers
There's no dearth of murderous dancers
But a well wisher says all the best
May you overcome all your tests
Many challenges you will face
But America surely has risen above race
Barack Obama is your name
Finally you are free from chains

Designs

As I stood and swore
My feelings I ignored
I did not mourn
Did not groan
At the severing of ties
Did not think twice
For the relationship to India will never be broken
Will be there in my emotions unspoken
Perhaps partly in the way I see things
But I realized the responsibility citizenship brings
I felt touched by the way I had been allowed
And solemnly I vowed
Some had gone through the same process
Masquerading as British citizens, no less
And had struck mercilessly
Shamelessly
The portrayal
Of Betrayal
Indians have served this land
This nation grand
Without deceiving
Giving but also receiving
Politeness and kindness
And love, no less
And hopefully will continue to do so
The relationship will fruitfully grow
As long as the separatist minds
Do not succeed in their malicious designs

Mishaps

Those children not allowed to be born
Not permitted to see the dawn
Was the world deprived of another Einstein
Would he or she shine
Could there have been another Picasso
We shall never know
But without going into the wrong or the right
One thinks of those who did not see light
Were they better off perhaps
For they avoided life's inevitable mishaps
Never did they taste worry or grief
Never did they harbour dubious beliefs

Dad

I love you, I always have
I can never bear to see you sad
I remember how you never failed
To reward 'very goods' with tales
I remember how you patted my back
Whenever I was on the right track
I remember how you inspired me before every test
Encouraged me to do my best
I remember the cups of tea together
I remember your conversations clever
How you discussed politics, literature, science
How you quoted famous writers' lines
I remember the smile on your face
I even remember the rainy days
I remember how you made me laugh and grin
How you forgave my loony sins
How you were always there for me
In your shade may I always be
Although we are miles apart
Of you, I'll always be a part
From the roof tops I will shout
The world's best dad without a doubt

Sigh

An argument for many years has baffled
The answer never fully unravelled
Are we God's creation
Or is God our creation
Absence of evidence
Is not evidence of absence
The believers argue
With their religious hue
The atheist disagrees
God he cannot see
Should one acknowledge
Accept His message
Or should one deny
Some think with a sigh
Does faith have to be without question
Doubts not mentioned

Names

Bewitchingly beautiful, innocently divine
Vivacious, bubbly, not yet nine
Jet black hair, a face uniquely rare
Sparkling eyes that tell no lies
A sweet little nose, it is perfect so
Lips so pink they make you blink
Oblivious to her obvious loveliness
Even in childhood, she has finesse
She prattles and chatters
About things that matter
She is laughter, she is sunshine
Doesn't matter if she isn't mine
Suddenly she sulks and shuts up
Until gently her cheeks I rub
Within a moment she dispels the gloom
And all around the world roses bloom
Our earth is full of such lovely little dames
Whatever their appearance, whatever their names

Dwell

Socially awkward
Like a lost little bird
I always endeavour to fit in
With my silly smiles and foolish grins
Trying to be what people want me to be
And losing in the process, that which is me
I feel I am playing house
To now, I should bow
I am in a cage
On the same page
Why can't I break my shell
In what world do I dwell

Exceptions

One hears of chilling crimes
With almost an immune mind
Both in other places and here
One feels perhaps a pinch of fear
Sometimes one is totally indifferent
The victim seems a number, not significant
Without going into the tales sordid
And the nature horrid
One can clearly say
With a hint of dismay
Human nature is the same everywhere
Ghoulish minds don't care
Yet a lot of goodness goes unnoticed
Rays of sunshine penetrate the mist
Criminal exceptions do no not make the rule
A lot of kindness only a spot of cruel
Makes this world worth living in
Goodness overshadows sins
One thought we can perish
That the guilty will go unpunished

Rest

Should I forget you
And let you go
Should I release your hand
And footprints in the sand
Should I leave you
And say goodbye
Should I resist
From gazing in the mist
Should I forget your caress
And let you rest

I miss you

Little footsteps, I miss you
Curly hair, I miss you
Big brown eyes, I miss you
Shaky laughter, I miss you
Silly jokes, I miss you
Come home son, I miss you

Feverish frenzy

Imagination runs riot
While the night is quiet
Creative urges come tip toe
As beside me you snore
Past and present blend
Will thoughts never end
Rainbow colours in my mind
With their ferocity are turning me blind
Darkness lingers on
As my dazzling mind shone
In my bed I toss and turn
The flame of passion burns and burns
The glitter of thoughts is too much to take
This here is my sanity at stake
This feverish frenzy ignites
Takes me to colossal heights
I will leap up and grab the sky
Yes, I admit, I'm high
From the so- called normal I deviate
Soon they will have reason to sedate

Hoard

As I walk on my chosen road
My memories I hoard
It is a big load
As I walk on my road
It has got joy, it has got sorrow too
A little chaos, impulses few
A lot of emotion
Some commotion
Stresses and pressures
A few treasures
Shrieks, arguments and fights
Situations tight
Some jokes
Shared with folks
An indiscretion or two
Regrets few
I squint to see
I try to perceive
What lies ahead
Perhaps a rosy bed

Phantom

My love for you has never dwindled
In your absence, it has rekindled
My love for you is pure as the snow
Every day it grows and grows
My love for you is like a mirage
Yet it is painfully large
My love for you is discreet
It starts and ends at your street
My love for you is a phantom
Yet hard to abandon
My love for you is a rose without thorns
It is a dew- kissed morn
My love for you hasn't been without doubts
It's always been a whisper, never a shout
My love for you is platonic
Yet its effect is magic
My corpse of love for you still breathes
It is a shaking leaf
I might not even recognize you now
Yet to the love you stir, I still bow
My love for you has created boundaries for me
In every man, it is you I see
I pull myself away from the merest hint of a crush
Perhaps the field of my love is still green and lush

Door

I sat waiting for my husband in hospital
The weather was painfully dismal
Grey was the sky
And I sighed
The door swung open again and again
And brought in the chilling wind of Britain
An English lady at the reception
Understood the situation
Took the trouble to notice
And I must say this
She came out and made sure
That the cold I would not endure
The door she closed
Like a gracious host
Who was I to her
That her feelings I stirred
We were not related by blood
I was a lotus, she a rose bud
Yet she cared, cared enough
To shield me against the cold and rough
The country suddenly seemed very warm to me
For it is inhabited by many like she
The weather didn't matter any more
As I looked at the closed door

Never a tear

What would life be without romance
Without the uncertainty of chance
What would life be without those thoughts
If we questioned everything we sought
What is life without fire
What would life be without desire
Without the trembling of a racing heart
If lovers always met, never had to part
What would a rose be without its thorns
If there was only the dazzle of dawn
If there were only smiles, never a tear
And never the longing of someone dear
What would life be without a leafless tree
If we never had sorrow, just pure glee
If every day was sunny and clear
If we weren't mortals mere
With joy, why be sedated
Happiness is overrated

Stilled

Seeds of thoughts are born in me
The seeds take roots
They grow shoots and leaves
They grow flowers
Will the thoughts I cherish
One day perish
Will the thoughts breed
And give rise to more
And anyway, do thoughts count
Or should they be pushed back
Into the grey area they have emerged from
To be stilled for ever
To raise their heads never

Tree

I remember that tree with yellow flowers
Looking lovely beneath the stars
I remember how I gazed
Drunk with its beauty, with admiration laced
I remember as the flowers fell on us
Without a sound, without a fuss
I remember my dad calling the flower gold
To that idea, I was sold
I remember sitting there on a garden chair
Without a worry, without a care
The house that was ours, yet not ours at all
I remember the things, big and small
Someone else must be sitting there now
Sighing at nature's loveliness, saying Wow
For a while that house was mine
Its memories in my own ways I signed
I think of the earth as my own
For a while call it home
Yet one day it'll belong to another
But it makes me smile, not shiver or shudder
Knowing this truth, we still strive till the end
To the world, our images we lend
Yet that's how it should be
Says that sweet massive tree

Mine

Sometimes I wonder where you are
As I think of you from afar
Are you stealing hearts still
Attracting Sheela, enticing Jill
A touch of grey probably in your hair
A hint of danger in your stare
Have your lost weight or put on some
Are you happy or are you glum
Thinking nothing happened, wishing something had
Does the perusal of the past make you sad
Do you still possess that mischievous grin
Do you think of the silliness that I had been
Do you sometimes lie awake in bed
Thinking of all that we never said
Do you then shrug off the feeling like I do
Do you ever wonder if my love was true
Do you still dress just the same
Do you even remember my name
Do you wish we had stumbled on slippery slopes
Do you still dream and hope
Do you think of me as I think of you
Do you mention me when you've had a few
Do you still walk on that road
Like some poet's ode
Do you smile not knowing the effect it has
Do you think of me as a foolish lass
Are you as baffled as me as to what it all was
Do you stop to think and pause
Do you even have the time
To linger in the past like these lingering thoughts of mine

Home

If only the kiss of life
Could bring back those who died
If only we could go back in time
Erase insensitive words and lines
If only we could banish the laziness which stopped us helping a loved one
If only we had showered those times with fun
If only we had known the person would be gone
We would have rid them of their sorrowful thorns
If only we'd known, if only
Our memories wouldn't be so lonely
If only God would be so kind
As to read our minds
If only God's heart wasn't made of stone
And He'd bring back the dead walking home

Tempted

You looked at me with those eyes of yours
And I was tempted to break all rules and laws
I was tempted to throw caution to the wind
I was tempted to smile and grin
I was tempted to do all that was wrong
To write to you a letter long
I was tempted to risk all I had
I was tempted not to be sad
I was tempted to cross barriers and lines
I was tempted to make you mine
I was tempted to stoop very low
Just because I loved you so
I was tempted by your air of menace
For goodness I couldn't care less
I was tempted to give you a call
To announce my love to one and all
I was tempted to scribble your name
In my diary on every page
I was tempted to fly in the sky
I was tempted to look you right in the eye
I was tempted to go to your house
But I've always been a frightened mouse
I was tempted, I was tempted so
I was tempted, I'll have you know
Maybe it is much better this way
Maybe it's better I had no say
There's something reassuring about a dull life
For excitement I will not strive
I'd rather have no surprises and shocks
I'd rather have a dependable rock
But I was tempted, this is no joke
For you were my kind of bloke
You definitely were my cup of tea
But I'll forget you, I'll let you be

Roses

The roses have finally said goodbye
The petals are now beginning to sigh
We died, they say a long time ago
But it's now our demise really shows
Killed for your sense of beauty and pleasure
Our death has become your temporary treasure
The water in the vase
Is a pretence, it is a farce
Stop this charade of keeping me alive
This illusion of making me thrive
You know as well as I
It is a sham, it is a lie
The loveliness you see
Is not really me
How I always dreaded Valentine's Day
My looks a re a curse, I must say
To portray your love, I gave up my life
Stop using me, all you romantic guys
Love can be momentary just like me
Surely you see that, surely you see

Ties

There he goes selecting a tie again
Oh men, these dithering men
He looks at the blue, red and green
In clumsy attire, he refuses to be seen
The trousers for tomorrow are spread out on the bed
In a not matching shirt, he wouldn't be caught dead
Much deliberation, after much careful thought
He tries to decide what he ought
If the shirt is plain, the tie can be designed
He really can't seem to make up his mind
A fetish for ties he possesses
Each of his three ties, he lovingly caresses
And to top it all
It's his downfall
That ties are going out of style
For hygiene, some are waving them goodbye
But on occasions he still wears his
I wouldn't be surprised if he gives it a kiss

Humour

I've always loved novels of Wodehouse
I loved them before and I love them now
Jeeves gives me more delight than he does Bertie
For a butler his books make me thirsty
O! To have a Jeeves about the house
I think as through his novels I browse
To be served breakfast in bed
To be listened to all I said
To hear his words, Certainly Mam
To be served bacon, eggs, bread and jam
To lean on him for my slightest disaster
To be in the presence of this brainy crafter
To be rolling in money like Bertie
Never to wash clothes dirty
Jeeves' flawless English still leaves me amazed
And I adore Bertie's silly ways
There is laughter in almost every other line
No wonder Wodehouse is a favourite of mine
It is a fact, it is no rumour
That Wodehouse is the best in humour
I'm sure millions others share my delight
Pip pip and toodle do we say to his might

The Bear

A bear may be dark, it may be pale
It has short furry ears and hardly any tail
Its feet are strong with five toes
Its coat may be thin or it may be coarse
It has powerful claws on its feet
It likes to eat vegetables and meat
It is no puzzle
It has a long muzzle

The Buffalo

Buffaloes may be wild or tame
If tame, they can be given a name
They try to avoid flies
They tend to lie
In water or in mud
They chew cud
Sometimes reddish, mostly black
If wounded, with horns they attack
Tame ones do a lot of work
Their work they do not shirk
They plough fields and pull carts
At this work, they are smart

The Camel

In its hump, the camel has fat
This fact ensures that
Without food and water it can survive
In deserts, it thrives
It can endure hardship
Of the desert it is the ship
It can carry heavy loads
On sandy, barren roads
Its lips are covered with thick, coarse hairs
So it can eat thorny shrubs with care
Bushy eyebrows, long lashes, hairy ear
From the sand keep it clear
It can close its nostrils in a sand storm
It can carry Jill, it can carry John
Its feet prevent it from sinking into sand
It is an animal, big and grand

The Cat

Belonging to the tiger and leopard clan
A tame cat can be a pet of man
Some cats, however are wild
Found in climate, tropical or mild
With whiskers, claws, usually a tail
A cat can be dark, it can be pale
A cat has strength, it has grace
It follows rats at a very fast pace
Better than us it can see in the dark
It is frightened of a dog's bark
It follows and jumps on its prey
It is dangerous in its own way-
Little birds in the garden
The cat refuses to pardon
When hungry or wanting petting, it miaows
Don't ask what, don't ask how
When petted, it purrs with joy
It waves its tail when annoyed
When frightened by a dog, it spits and hisses
It responds to love, it responds to kisses
It uses its teeth to tear, chop meat
It can be angry, it can be sweet

The Cheetah

It is well- known that
The cheetah belongs to the clan of the cat
The cheetah is more slender than a leopard
The cheetah is feared by shepherds
Compared to a leopard, its legs are longer
Difficult to say who is stronger
Unlike leopard's rosettes, its coat has single spots
In the past for its skin it was sought
Extremely fast, a sight to behold
The cheetah is daring and bold

The Donkey

An ass can be wild or tame
It is a donkey with a different name
Yes, it is different from a horse
This is simply, because
It is small and has smaller ears
And it is also quite clear
It has a tufted tail, narrow feet
It greets with a bray, not a neigh sweet
It also has a standing mane
But let's not view it with disdain
It may be grey or a different hue
It is different from a horse, it is true
An ass is very strong and hardy
On mountains it is quite sturdy

The Elephant

An elephant is big and stout
It is heavy without a doubt
The largest living land animal
It carries loads like a camel
It is also quite clear
It has two large flopping ears
It has a small brain and tiny eyes
Perhaps small for its size
Long and slender is its tail
Its skin is grey, not light or pale
Its four legs are stocky and short
Most have tusks, some do not
What really draws it apart
Is its trunk, an amazing part
An elephant's trunk is really long
It is an animal strong
Its trunk it uses as arms, nose and lips
With its trunk, things it grips
It really is a shame
Sometimes it suffered pain
Hunters were seen to be thrilled
As for its ivory tusk they killed
An elephant can be wild or tame
It is loved by Tom, it is loved by Jane

The Fox

A fox is often followed by hounds
Its home is 'earth' in the ground
It hunts birds, frogs and mice
It is an animal, cunning and wise
It eats worms and berries it can find
Of foxes there are many different kinds
It is no puzzle
It has bright eyes and a sharp muzzle
It has pointed ears and a bushy tail
It can be red, silver, it can be pale
To escape from hounds, it pretends to be dead
Thus a fox is clever, be it silver or red

The Frog

Frogs live in water and on land
Frogs are small, not very grand
Frogs can be of different kinds
Frogs have long hinds
Frog's skin is usually smooth and shiny
Most frogs feed on insects and worms tiny
Nearly all frogs have teeth
They have a special method to breathe
Bigger animals make frogs their prey
So frogs defend themselves in their own way
The poison glands in their skin
Against foes sometimes make them win
Eggs, tadpole and frog are their three stages
Description of frogs can fill pages

The Giraffe

The giraffe is the tallest animal
It is an African mammal
Its back slopes downwards towards the tail
The female giraffe is shorter than the male
It is not wrong
To say its neck and legs are long
Although the giraffe is very tall
Its head is narrow and small
When a giraffe we watch
We notice its colouring is splotched
It is not wrong
To say its tail is long
When drinking its head stoops
It likes to live in groups
When attacked it gallops very fast
For its hide, it was hunted in the past
The giraffe eats not grass but leaves
The giraffe is liked by Jane, by Steve

The Goat

Milk provides a goat
Leather and cloth is made of its coat
Its hooves are divided into two
It is seen that the cud it chews
It is not very weird
That most have a beard
It has a turned- up short tail
It can be dark, it can be pale
Both males and females have horns
For protection, like a rose's thorns

The Gorilla

The gorilla is a heavy animal
It is true it is a mammal
It has deep set eyes and flaring nostrils
It can live in lowlands, mountains or hills
Its ears are a reasonable size
It is an animal very wise
When threatened, a male beats his chest with his hands
It makes a display, aggressive and grand
After that, it generally retreats
It likes to eat plants and rarely touches meat
The gorilla is in some ways like a man
Liked by Julie, it is loved by Dan

The Hamster

Sometimes kept as pet animals
A hamster is a stocky little mammal
For this fact I can vouch
Each cheek has a pouch
And it has been found
It makes its home under the ground
It has black shiny eyes and a very short tail
A hamster can be female, it can be male
Storing food is its habit
It lives in burrows like a rabbit
As it eats fruits, vegetables and grain
It can be a pest, it can be a pain
A hamster has its woes
Owls, weasels and hawks are his foes

The Horse

Handsome, graceful is a horse
A horse has fought many wars
Running on its four single toes
It flees away from its foes
A horse has special needs
It can be found in many breeds
It helps in transport like a camel
It is a valued, useful mammal
All horses are not the same
All horses are not tame
A baby horse is called a foal
Mares and stallions play many roles
Not just in war and transport
They also play a part in sports
Polo is one of them
In racing, they are prized as gems
Many a race has been won and lost
By one gallop, by one trot
Used on ranches and for pleasure
A horse can be a tamed treasure

The Kangaroo

It is indeed very true
An unusual creature is a kangaroo
There are many different kinds
With short front legs and powerful hinds
A kangaroo is seen to slouch
Mother carries her young in a pouch
At 6 months, the baby's head sticks out
Pulling leaves from branches thin and stout
Wonder where kangaroo is found
Hopping along on the ground?

The Leopard

It is quite well- known that
A leopard belongs to the clan of the cat
His coat can be yellowish- brown with black spots
He is hidden, not easy to spot
Baboons and antelopes are his favourite prey
He raids villages for goats some days
He is quite at home in trees
Lying among the many leaves
From the trees he jumps on monkey and deer
One thing should be made clear
Is demand for his fur illegal?
Isn't this an animal regal!

The Lion

O! The lion's golden mane
Makes it the favourite of Jill and Jane
Oh! The lion's frightening roar
It frightens the bear, it scares the boar
It is the king, unlike the rest
It lives in a den, not in a burrow or nest
In its strength lies its beauty
To preserve it is our duty
So believe me friends, it is no jest
It is the lion that I love the best

The Mongoose

The mongoose is a small animal
It is true it is a mammal
It is like a ferret in shape and size
It is sharp- sighted, it is wise
The mongoose has a long pointed nose
Its fur is often rough, of course
The mongoose feeds on rats, worms and snails
It is true it has a tail
It eats fruits and vegetables
To kill snakes, it is sometimes capable

The Monkey

The monkey is a hairy animal
It is true that he is a mammal
The monkey is found in a warm climate
Like man, he belongs to order Primate
The monkey usually lives in trees
He apes you, he apes me
The monkey has mostly not claws but nails
He also happens to have a tail
The monkey belongs to the ape clan
In some ways he is similar to man

The Pig

We all very well know
On each foot a pig has four toes
Pigs are truly quite stout
They have strong snouts
With the snout roots they dig
There are many breeds of pigs
Pigs are often kept in sties
The sty should be warm and dry
Very quickly sows reproduce
Little piglets they produce
Besides tame, there are wild pigs too
Of pigs, there are kinds quite a few

The Rabbit

Hopping seems his habit
He is a rabbit
In the jungles he does roam
Makes a burrow his happy home
If he happens to be tame
You can give him any name
How many kinds? There are eighteen
Eating grass and barks is his routine
Foxes, hawks and weasels are his foes
A male is a buck, a female a doe
A short tail or scut he possesses
He responds to caresses

The Rat

Most people do not like rats
Rats are pounced upon by cats
Rats are found almost everywhere
Can be tiny as a mouse, or big as a hare
Rats do damage by eating food
They gnaw through pipes in a manner crude
Rats can be black or brown
Live in villages, live in towns
Rats make all the mischief they can make
They used to spread a disease called plague
It is well- known that
Owls and hawks eat rats
Against rats we have constant war
Rats however continue to gnaw
Painless poisons are used to kill rats
Rats are petrified of cats
White rats are often searched
For use as pets and scientific research
Thus rats can be a menace, it is true
But in a scientific way, they are useful too

The Sheep

A sheep is related to the goat
But unlike the goat, it has a woolly coat
Unlike lions that live in dens
Tame sheep can be kept in a pen
Male sheep are called rams, female ewes
Sheep come in colours quite a few
Tame sheep graze in fields on summer days
In winter, in pens, they are fed on hay
Besides tame, there are wild sheep too
Breeds of sheep there are quite a few
Sheep are hoofed, cud- chewing mammals
Unlike goats they are beard- less animals

The Squirrel

Nuts and birds' eggs he nibbles
He is a squirrel
There are many different kinds
In most places they are easy to find
They are different from a rabbit
They vary in colour, size and habit
They may be red, black or grey
They are interesting in their own way
It is well- known that
They like to gnaw like rats
Their bushy tails are usually long
And thus ends the squirrel's song

The Tiger

The tiger moves softly over twigs
He hunts fish, he hunts pigs
Sometimes the tiger hunts on goats
He has an orange and black striped coat
The tiger catches his prey by the throat and shoulder
As his hunger smoulders
If sick or old, he may kill a man
The tiger belongs to the cat clan
Sadly, hunters were seen to gloat
As they killed him for sport and coat

The Wolf

Wolves live in groups or packs
Birds and deer they attack
Wolves attack domestic livestock
Wolves live in lairs or among rocks
Where their prey is, they can tell
By their keen sense of smell
In hot plains and barren grounds they prowl
Wolves do not bark, they howl
In the spring wolf cubs are born
They're found in climate, cold and warm
If hungry or threatened, wolves can
Sometimes ferociously attack man
Sadly, because wolves attacked cattle
Hunters against wolves waged a battle

The Zebra

Zebras can be of different types
Zebras have black and white stripes
The mountain zebra is very rare
Other kinds of zebras are also there
Moving in herds, they are lions' prey
Some extinct ones were found to neigh
For hide and flesh, some were shot by man
Zebras belong to the horse clan
Wonder where zebras are found?
Wonder where zebras abound?

About the Author

Seema Jha a British Indian woman lives in Boston,Lincolnshire,U.K. Married to a consultant psychiatrist she is blessed with a son.Born in India ,she migrated to U.K in 1995 with her family. Her first published work is a collection of poems called 'Of Mauves and Oranges'